Instant Memories™

LOVE

READY-TO-USE SCRAPBOOK PAGES

Nancy Rosin

Sterling Publishing Co., Inc. New York
A Sterling/Chapelle Book

Author: Nancy Rosin

If you have any questions or comments, please contact:
Chapelle, Ltd., Inc., P.O. Box 9252, Ogden, UT 84409
(801) 621-2777 • (801) 621-2788 Fax
e-mail: chapelle@chapelleltd.com
Web site: www.chapelleltd.com

Instant Memories is a trademark of Sterling Publishing Co., Inc.

PC Configuration with 128 MB Ram or greater. At least 100 MB of free hard disk space. Dual speed or faster CD-ROM drive, and a 24-bit color monitor.

Macintosh Configuration with 128 MB Ram or greater. At least 100 MB of free hard disk space. Dual speed or faster CD-ROM drive, and a 24-bit color monitor.

10 9 8 7 6 5 4 3 2 1

Published by Sterling Publishing Co., Inc.
387 Park Avenue South, New York, NY 10016
© 2005 by Sterling Publishing Co., Inc.
Distributed in Canada by Sterling Publishing
c/o Canadian Manda Group, 165 Dufferin Street
Toronto, Ontario, Canada M6K 3H6
Distributed in Great Britain by Chrysalis Books Group PLC,
The Chrysalis Building, Bramley Road, London W10 6SP, England
Distributed in Australia by Capricorn Link (Australia) Pty. Ltd.
P. O. Box 704, Windsor, NSW 2756, Australia
Printed and Bound in China
All Rights Reserved

Sterling ISBN 1-4027-2642-2

For information about custom editions, special sales, premium and corporate purchases, please contact Sterling Special Sales Department at 800-805-5489 or specialsales@sterlingpub.com.

Introduction

Scrapbooking is a wonderful way to document special day-to-day events, holidays, celebrations, and family history. However, not everyone has the time or the money to do what it takes to create show-stopping scrapbook pages. That's where the *Instant Memories™ Ready-to-Use Scrapbook Page* series comes in. The top designers in the field have done all the work for you—simply add your favorite photos to their layouts and you're done! Or add a few embellishments, such as a charm or ribbon, and you have a unique personalized page in minutes. You can tear the pages directly from the book, photocopy them to use time and again, or print them from the enclosed CD.

As an added bonus in the *Instant Memories* series, we have included hundreds of rare, vintage images on the enclosed CD-rom. From Victorian postcards to hand-painted beautiful borders and frames, it would take years to acquire a collection like this. However, with this easy-to-use resource, you'll have them all right here, right now, to use for any computer project over and again. Each image has been reproduced to the highest quality standard for photocopying and scanning and can be reduced or enlarged to suit your needs.

Perfect for paper crafting, scrapbooking, and fabric transfers, *Instant Memories* books will inspire you to explore new avenues of creativity. We've included a sampling of ideas to get you started, but the best part is using your imagination to create your own projects. Be sure to look for other books in this series as we continue to search the markets for wonderful vintage images.

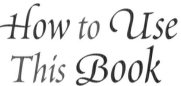

How to Use This Book

General Instructions:

The art pages in this book are printed on one side only, making it easy to simply tear out the pages and use as is, or if you choose, you can cut out individual images to use on our own pages and projects. However, you'll probably want to use them again, so the enclosed CD-Rom contains all of the images individually as well as in the page layout form. The images are large enough to use at 12" x 12". The CDs can be used with both PC and Mac formats. Just pop in the disk. On a PC, the file will immediately open to the Home page, which will walk you through how to view and print the images. For Macintosh users, you will simply double-click on the icon to open. The images may also be incorporated into your computer projects using simple imaging software that you can purchase specifically for this purpose—a perfect choice for digital scrapbooking.

The reference numbers printed on the back of each image in the book are the same ones used on the CD, which will allow you to easily find the image you are looking for. The numbering consists of the book abbreviation, the page number, the image number, and the file format. The first file number (located next to the page number) is for the entire page. For example, LOV01-01.jpg would be the entire image for page 1 of Love. The second file number is for the top-right image. The numbers continue in a counterclockwise spiral fashion.

Once you have resized your images, added text, created a scrapbook page, etc., you are ready to print them. Printing on cream or white cardstock, particularly a textured variety, creates a more authentic look. You won't be able to tell that it's a reproduction! If you don't have access to a computer or printer, that's ok. Most photocopy centers can resize and print your images for a nominal fee, or they have do-it-yourself machines that are easy to use.

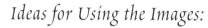

Ideas for Using the Images:

Scrapbooking: These images are perfect for both heritage and modern scrapbook pages. Simply use the image as a frame, accent piece, or border. For those of you with limited time, the page layouts in this book have been created so that you can use them as they are. Simply print out or photocopy the desired page, attach a photograph into one of the boxes, add your own journaling, and you have a beautiful designer scrapbook page in minutes. Be sure to print your images onto acid-free cardstock so the pages will last a lifetime.

Cards: Some computer programs allow images to be inserted into a card template, simplifying cardmaking. If this is not an option, simply use the images as accent pieces on the front or inside of the card. Use a bone folder to score the card's fold to create a more professional look.

Decoupage/Collage Projects: For decoupage or collage projects, photocopy or print the image onto a thinner paper such as copier paper. Thin paper adheres to projects more effectively. Decoupage medium glues and seals the project, creating a gloss or matte finish when dry, thus protecting the image. Vintage images are beautiful when decoupaged to cigar boxes, glass plates, and even wooden plaques. The possibilities are endless.

Fabric Arts: Vintage images can be used in just about any fabric craft imaginable: wall hangings, quilts, bags, or baby bibs. Either transfer the image onto the fabric by using a special iron-on paper, or by printing the image directly onto the fabric, using a temporary iron-on stabilizer that stabilizes the fabric to feed through a printer. These items are available at most craft and sewing stores. If the item will be washed, it is better to print directly on the fabric. For either method, follow the instructions on the package.

Wood Transfers: It is now possible to print images on wood. Use this exciting technique to create vintage plaques, clocks, frames, and more. A simple, inexpensive transfer tool is available at most large craft or home improvement stores, or online from various manufacturers. You simply place the photocopy of the image you want, face down, onto the surface and use the tool to transfer the image onto the wood. This process requires a copy from a laser printer, which means you will probably have to get your copies made at a copy center. Refer to manufacturer's instructions for additional details. There are other transfer products available that can be used with wood. Choose the one that is easiest for you.

Gallery of Ideas

These *Love* images can be used in a variety of projects; cards, scrapbook pages, and decoupage projects to name a few. The images can be used as they are shown in the layout, or you can copy and clip out individual images, or even portions or multitudes of images. The following pages contain a collection of ideas to inspire you to use your imagination and create one-of-a-kind treasures.

Idea 1

As you can see below, it is very easy to simply place a photo into one of the frames and you have a beautiful finished scrapbook page. The addition of the velvet flowers adds that extra-special touch.

Art Page 30

Idea 2 — *I*f you are using an image that has buttons, charms, or ribbons already on it, attach a similar item—in this case the cord around the edge— over the image for added dimension and style.

Art Page 31

Idea 3

$\mathfrak{V}$intage pet images provide a great backdrop for scrapbook pages honoring our beloved pets. Add cherished pet tags or other items of remembrance.

George

1975 ~ 1995

With Our Love

Art Page 44

Idea 4 **N**otice how the burlap image was used on the
layouts above and at left—one as background for a
snippet of memorabilia and the other as a photo mat.

Art Page 45

Idea 5

$\mathfrak{T}$his laminated placemat would make a fun gift for a loved one. Select the desired images you want to use, along with some special photographs. Collage and seal your images within plastic sheets that come in laminate kits that are readily available at office supply, craft, or copy centers.

Idea 6

This heart shaped treasure box is adorned with color-copied images and Dresden metallic edging along the base and lid. Incorporating personal photographs into the design results in even more sentimentality.

Idea 7 **N**otice how bits of lace, ribbon, and flowers alter this scrapbook page into something that should be framed and treasured for years to come.

Art Page 2

Idea 8   𝔙intage images are perfect for decoupaging. This heart-shaped box, coated in silver glitter, displays an image framed by antique flowers and leaves.

Idea 9

𝖂hen printing out your images, make two or three copies. This allows you to layer the images between foam dots and create a beautiful dimensional image.

Idea 10

𝔜ou can create hundreds of one-of-a-kind greeting cards using the images provided in this book. Trim your cards with vintage-looking elements for an elegant finish.

LOV01-02

LOV01-03

LOV01-04

1 ─| LOV01-01 |

LOV02-03

LOV02-02

LOV02-04

LOV02-05

LOV02-06

LOV02-01   2

This Certifies

That on the _____ day of _____

IN THE YEAR OF OUR LORD _____

and _____ is _____

_____ were by me united in

MARRIAGE

at _____

according to the Laws of the State of _____

Witnesses

SILVER WEDDING.

Mr. & Mrs. A. J. Levy,

AT HOME,

1843   1868

Thursday Even'g, Dec. 31, '68,

No. 95 Barr St., Cincinnati, O.

A. J. LEVY   HENRIETTA LEVY

SILVER WEDDING.

Mr. & Mrs. A. J. Levy,

1843, 1868,

LOV03-03   LOV03-02

                                            LOV03-07

                    LOV03-04   LOV03-05   LOV03-06

3 — LOV03-01

LOV04-03

LOV04-02

LOV04-07

LOV04-06

LOV04-04

LOV04-05

LOV04-01 | 4

WITH EVERY LOVING WISH FOR YOUR BIRTHDAY

MANY HAPPY RETURNS OF THE DAY

A HAPPY BIRTHDAY

LOV05-02

LOV05-03

LOV05-08

LOV05-04　　　LOV05-09

LOV05-07

LOV05-05

LOV05-06

5 ─| LOV05-01 |

LOV06-02

LOV06-04   LOV06-03

LOV06-05

LOV06-06

LOV06-01 — **6**

My
Valentine
think of me

LOV07-03

LOV07-02

LOV07-04

LOV07-05

LOV07-06

7 — LOV07-01

LOV08-04

LOV08-03

LOV08-02

LOV08-05

LOV08-09

LOV08-08

LOV08-06

LOV08-07

LOV08-01 8

MATERNITY

LOV09-04

LOV09-03

LOV09-02

LOV09-05

LOV09-08

LOV09-06

LOV09-07

9 LOV09-01

LOV10-02

LOV10-06

LOV10-03

LOV10-05

LOV10-04

LOV10-01 — **10**

WITH MY LOVE.

A road to
a *friend's* house
is never long.

—Danish Proverb

Friendships
are fragile things, and require
as much handling as any other
fragile and *precious* thing.

—Randolph S. Bourne

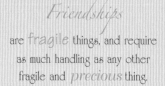

LOV11-02

LOV11-03   LOV11-09

LOV11-04

LOV11-05   LOV11-10

LOV11-06

LOV11-08

LOV11-07

11 — LOV11-01

LOV12-03

LOV12-02

LOV12-04

LOV12-07

LOV12-06

LOV12-05

LOV12-01 — **12**

As the stars in their courses,
The tides of the sea,
Are constant and changeless,
So I am to thee.

With *Love* and *Best Wishes*.

LOV13-03   LOV13-02

LOV13-04

LOV13-05   LOV13-06   LOV13-07

13— LOV13-01

LOV14-04   LOV14-03   LOV14-02

LOV14-05

LOV14-10

LOV14-06   LOV14-09

LOV14-07   LOV14-08

LOV14-01 — **14**

Favorite Places:

Our Favorite Memory

I'll never forget...

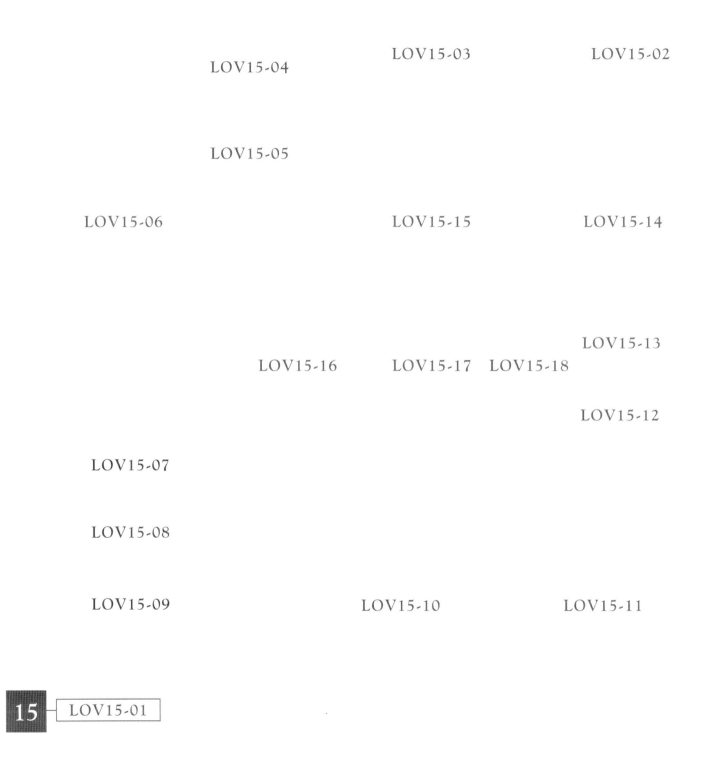

LOV15-04

LOV15-03

LOV15-02

LOV15-05

LOV15-06

LOV15-15

LOV15-14

LOV15-13

LOV15-16

LOV15-17

LOV15-18

LOV15-12

LOV15-07

LOV15-08

LOV15-09

LOV15-10

LOV15-11

15 LOV15-01

LOV16-05   LOV16-04   LOV16-03   LOV16-02

LOV16-06   LOV16-10   LOV16-09

LOV16-08

LOV16-07

LOV17-05   LOV17-04   LOV17-03   LOV17-02

LOV17-06

LOV17-10

LOV17-09

LOV17-07   LOV17-08

17 — LOV17-01

LOV18-05   LOV18-04   LOV18-03   LOV18-02

LOV18-06

LOV18-10

LOV18-07

LOV18-09

LOV18-08   LOV18-01 — **18**

Valentine Greetings for YOU

LOV19-03   LOV19-02

LOV19-04

LOV19-08   LOV19-07

LOV19-05   LOV19-06

LOV20-04　　　　LOV20-03　　　　LOV20-02

LOV20-05　　　　　　　　　LOV20-06

LOV20-01 20

A VALENTINE to my SWEETHEART in the Service

LOV21-03   LOV21-02

                              LOV21-07

LOV21-04

                         LOV21-06

LOV21-05

LOV21-01

LOV22-05   LOV22-04   LOV22-03   LOV22-02

LOV22-06

LOV22-12   LOV22-11

LOV22-10

LOV22-07   LOV22-08   LOV22-09

LOV22-01 — 22

To my best Love.

A Token of Love

WITH MY LOVE

Oh come and sail away with me,
On the sea of love divine,
For a compass true
Your heart will do,
On the love-ship Valentine.

TO MY SWEET VALENTINE.

Sailor Cupid

I'm your Valentine

"I think I'll anchor right here!"

LOV23-04   LOV23-03   LOV23-02

LOV23-05

LOV23-11   LOV23-10

LOV23-06   LOV23-07   LOV23-08   LOV23-09

23 — LOV23-01

LOV24-03

LOV24-02

LOV24-08

LOV24-07

LOV24-04

LOV24-05

LOV24-06

LOV24-01

Sheltered in a wedding bower,
Love shall pass full many an hour,
Hyacinths and roses sweet,
Every sense shall charm and greet,
We will have so fond and true,
Hardi-case all I find in you.
Loving thus with ardor free,
Thus I plight my truth to thee.

Peerless

Bought of

THIS INVOICE
IS NET 30 DAYS.
1½ 2% 10 DAYS.

APARTMENTS
to let.
GRATIS
enquire within

Baltimore,

To DUFUR & C⁰

WIRE RAILING AND
ORNAMENTAL WIRE WORKS,
No. 36
North Howard Street.

Counter Railing No 2. 1¼ mesh ⅛ wire @ 60°
each   brackets   and Arch bar   30%

50
20
2

With drum, fife and fiddle three cupids advance,
And near a neat villa they play,
Reminding their votaries living within,
That this is SALE VALENTINE'S day
Permit me dear Madam; this wish to express,
Since I think the fit season has come:
That now I may have for my partner in life,
And a villa like this for my home.

MARCUS WARD & C⁰.

LOV25-03

LOV25-02

LOV25-04

LOV25-05

LOV25-06

LOV25-07

25 — LOV25-01

LOV26-03

LOV26-02

LOV26-06

LOV26-04

LOV26-05

LOV26-01 — 26

THE LITTLE GIFT I OFFER THEE,
IS ALL I HAVE TO SEND,
ACCEPT IT, DEAREST, THEN FROM ME,
AS COMING FROM A FRIEND.

LOV27-03

LOV27-02

LOV27-04

LOV27-05

LOV27-08

LOV27-06

LOV27-07

27 — LOV27-01

LOV28-02

LOV28-03

LOV28-04

LOV28-01 28

THE
ALT
LOV

Then to the Altar will I bring
The fairest roses of the morn
And of her flowers bereave the spring
Thy hallowed Temples to adorn.
Then to my wishes gentle youth incline
And take O take me for your Valentine.

The blushing rose that hangs its head
Or meets the sun with shrinking dread
Conceals with its heart a flame
Which from that glowing noontide came

BANK of TRUE LOVE

50   **50**

STATE OF MATRIMONY

(SECURED)
BY THE
PLEDGE
OF THE

FIDELITY.

I have I loved: but some strange spell
Forbids my heart its tale to tell,
Here, take this simple rose, and feel
The love my lips dare not reveal.

LOV29-03

LOV29-02

LOV29-04

LOV29-05

LOV29-06

LOV29-07

29 — LOV29-01

LOV30-04

LOV30-03

LOV30-02

LOV30-05

LOV30-01 30

LOV31-03

LOV31-02

LOV31-04

LOV31-05

31 — LOV31-01

LOV32-03

LOV32-02

LOV32-04

LOV32-06

LOV32-05

LOV32-01 32

Love come to yonder happy home.
A home prepared for thee,
Where naught but joy and pleasure.
Awaits both thee and me.

PROPOSAL.

Oh, lady! there be many things
That seem right fair above,
But sure not one among them all
Is half so sweet as love;—
Let us not pay our vows alone,
But join two altars into one.

A good wife makes a good husband.

When the Morn shines we'll haste away,
And shun the light of glaring day;
We'll plan the time & name the hour,
When we will grace Loves fairy bower.
Uniting in Loves marriage band,
Cupid & Hymen hand in hand.
Blest in each other, we'll incline
To give praise to St Valentine.

Ah to my bosom thou art dear
More dear than words can tell,
And if a fault is cherish'd there,
'Tis loving thee to well.

How wearily, oh how wearily drags life
Not more fair the valley treasure,
Nor more sweet the lily blows.
unsoothed by Love.

Then come the wild weather,
Come sleet or come snow;
We will stand by each other,
However it blow.

LOV33-03 LOV33-02

LOV33-04

LOV33-05

LOV33-08

LOV33-07

LOV33-06

33 — LOV33-01

LOV34-03

LOV34-02

LOV34-06

LOV34-04

LOV34-05

LOV34-01 34

THE MAGIC GLASS.

In yonder glass our happy fate descry;
Nor question further our blest destiny;
Tho' long neglected, & tho' long denied,
See there a happy youth & willing bride.

Tis true that thy accents which, present, I hear,
Are sweet as is sweetly-breathed music to ear;
While absence gives birth to a tear or a sigh,
In a moment they flee, when my fair one is by.

My vow I have registered, ever to prove
True, constant, sincere, and faithful in love;
I ask in return, but the wish to enshrine
The prayer of my heart on the tablet of thine!

The sun's a bridegroom,
earth a bride;
Sing heigh-ho!
They court from morn till eventide.
The earth shall pass, but love abide.
Sing heigh-ho and heigh-ho!
Young maids must marry.

C. Kingsley

With my love.

LOV35-03   LOV35-02

LOV35-04

LOV35-05   LOV35-06

35 — LOV35-01

LOV36-03   LOV36-02

LOV36-04

LOV36-07

LOV36-05

LOV36-06

LOV36-01 36

To my
Love

With
Best
Wishes

Token
of
Love

My
Sweetheart

LOV37-03

LOV37-02

LOV37-04

LOV37-05

LOV37-06

LOV37-01

LOV38-03

LOV38-02

LOV38-04

LOV38-06

LOV38-05

LOV38-01 38

LOV39-03

LOV39-02

LOV39-04

LOV39-06

LOV39-01

LOV39-05

LOV40-03

LOV40-02

LOV40-05

LOV40-04

LOV40-01 40

To my Favorite.

I love you.

LOV41-03

LOV41-02

LOV41-04

LOV41-08

LOV41-09

LOV41-05

LOV41-07

LOV41-06

41 — LOV41-01

LOV42-01

LOV43-02

LOV43-03

LOV43-04

LOV43-05   LOV43-06   LOV43-07

43 — LOV43-01

LOV44-04

LOV44-03

LOV44-02

LOV44-05

LOV44-06

LOV44-01 44

LOV45-03

LOV45-02

LOV45-04

LOV45-06

LOV45-05

45 — LOV45-01

LOV46-03

LOV46-02

LOV46-04

LOV46-05

LOV46-01 46

.TO.
MY LOVE

.TO.
MY LOVE

LOV47-03

LOV47-02

LOV47-04

LOV47-05

47 — LOV47-01

LOV48-07   LOV48-06   LOV48-05   LOV48-04   LOV48-03   LOV48-02

LOV48-15

LOV48-08   LOV48-14   LOV48-13

LOV48-12

LOV48-09   LOV48-10   LOV48-11

LOV48-01   48

LOVE

AUBURN, N.Y.

HENRY TRAUB, JR.
HENRY TRAUB, JR.

M_____

To Henry Traub & Son, Dr.
Furniture, Carpets, Bedding, Toys,
BABY CARRIAGES, VELOCIPEDES AND EXPRESS WAGONS,
38 TO 48 GENESEE STREET,   OLD BAPTIST CHURCH.

FOURTH OF JULY GOODS A SPECIALTY.

LOVELAND POSTAGE
1
ONE SENT

LOVELAND POSTAGE
1

LOV49-05 LOV49-04 LOV49-03 LOV49-02

LOV49-11

LOV49-06

LOV49-07

LOV49-10

LOV49-08

LOV49-09

49 — LOV49-01

LOV50-02

LOV50-03

LOV50-04

LOV50-07

LOV50-05

LOV50-06

LOV50-01 **50**

CONSTANCY.

There is nothing but death
Our affections can sever,
And till life's latest breath
Love shall bind us for ever.

FROM THE GARDEN OF LOVE

ALL · HAIL · MY · LOVE

FIDELITY.

Each glittering star on high shall tell,
That since the hour when first I met thee,
Though others may have loved thee well,
Yet never did I once forget thee!

The Love I Prize.

'Tis not the lilly brow I prize,
Nor rose-ate cheeks, nor sunny eyes—
Enough of lillies and of roses;
A thousandfold more dear to me
The look that gentle love discloses—
That look which love alone can see.

I LOVE YOU

LOV51-03

LOV51-02

LOV51-04

LOV51-05

LOV51-07

LOV51-06

LOV52-02

LOV52-03

LOV52-07

LOV52-04

LOV52-06

LOV52-05

LOV52-01 52

Now if you love me, take your quill,
Or pencil—that will do,
Give verse, prose, picture, what you will,
I'll do as much for you.

Who the fond partner of each joy I feel?
Who? the partner of my sighs and tears;
Let this, my humble Valentine reveal,
That you're that partner of my hopes & fears.

LOV53-02

LOV53-03   LOV53-06

LOV53-04   LOV53-05

53 ─ LOV53-01

LOV54-04

LOV54-03

LOV54-02

LOV54-05

LOV54-08

LOV54-06

LOV54-07

LOV54-01 54

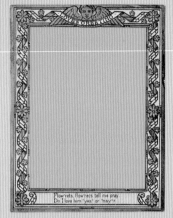

Flow'rets, flow'rets tell me pray.
Do I love him "yea" or "nay"?

LOVE'S GREETING

Flow'rets, flow'rets tell me pray.
Do I love him "yea" or "nay"?

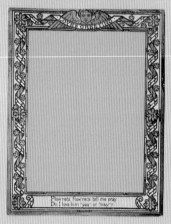

Flow'rets, flow'rets tell me pray.
Do I love him "yea" or "nay"?

To greet my Love.

LOVE'S GREETING

Flow'rets, flow'rets tell me pray.
Do I love him "yea" or "nay"?

To my Love.

Sweetheart think of me.

Sweetheart think of me.

LOV55-02

LOV55-03

LOV55-07

LOV55-04

LOV55-05

LOV55-06

LOV55-01

LOV56-04   LOV56-03   LOV56-02

LOV56-05

LOV56-07

LOV56-06

LOV56-01 — 56

MY HEART IS THINE.

Bid me die, or, if you will,
Cast me off, and that will kill;
But you cannot make me part
With the love within my heart.
Long that beating heart's been
    thine,
Take it for thy Valentine.

TO MY VALENTINE

Thou art the Star that guides me,
Thou art the sunbeam in the darkest hour,
Thou art the star that gilds life's dreary night,
Thou art the lovely little prison flower,
From gloom and sorrow turning to the light.
Then come to me; for O! my heart is aching
With a vain grief which I may not repress,
And ever there an earnest wish is waking
That thou wert here to soothe life's
loneliness.

THERE ARE MOMENTS
WE NEVER FORGET.

THERE ARE MOMENTS
WE NEVER FORGET.

LOV57-04   LOV57-03   LOV57-02

                                                     LOV57-08

           LOV57-05

                                                     LOV57-07

                 LOV57-06

57 — LOV57-01